Polishing Stone

Polishing Stone

The Collected Lyrics of GW Rasberry

Wintergreen Studios Press
Township of South Frontenac, PO Box 75, Yarker, ON, Canada K0K 3N0. Copyright © 2019 by Gary Rasberry. All rights reserved under the International and Pan-American Copyright Conventions. No part of this book may be reproduced in any form or by electronic or mechanical means, including information storage and retrieval systems, without permission in writing from the publisher, except by a reviewer, who may quote brief passages in a review. The views expressed in this work are those of the author and do not necessarily reflect those of the publisher.

Wintergreen Studios Press (WSP) gratefully acknowledges the financial support received from Wintergreen Studios.

Composed in Book Antiqua and Candara, typefaces designed by Monotype Typography and Gary Munch, respectively

Library and Archives Canada Cataloguing in Publication
Rasberry, Gary William. 1959 —
Polishing Stone/Gary Rasberry
ISBN: 978-1-989321-01-0

1. Poetry – Canadian.

   Title. Polishing Stone
   Legal Deposit – Library and Archives Canada

Other Books by Gary Rasberry

Some Days Just Noticing
Wintergreen Studios Press, 2016.

More Naked than Ever
Hidden Book Press, 2014.

As Though it Could be Otherwise
Studio 22 Idea Manufactory, 2012.

Writing Research/Researching Writing: Through a Poet's I.
Peter Lang, 2001.

Sixty Songs at Sixty

Much has been written about the Art & Science of Songwriting by songwriters far more prolific and prodigious than me. For this and other reasons, you will not find a treatise on songwriting here. What I can safely say is that the songs compiled in this volume are my own. But wait…perhaps not even this statement is entirely accurate? For as anyone who has ever tried a hand at songwriting knows, the song never truly belongs to the songwriter. This is not humility speaking. Songs are famous for "appearing" in such a way that the songwriter is often left slightly bedazzled. In this way, the process of writing a song is often and necessarily accorded upper case status, as in—The Mystery. Not to get too bogged down in semantics—I have certainly aspired to be a conduit for songs over the years. During this time, I have managed to write songs through some combination of stubbornness and tenacity and a willingness to risk being vulnerable enough to call what emerged from the process "a song." There have been moments of inspiration and insight, accompanied by bolts of lightning and other various and sundry pyrotechnics. There have also been moments of songwriting that are the equivalent of watching paint dry. Both kinds of songwriting are seemingly necessary if not compulsory.

Sixty Songs at Sixty. Aside from being attractively alliterative, this phrase provided enough of a spark to nudge me toward collecting lyrics to songs I've written over a number of years. It seemed a fair idea to gather and compile these lyrics during my sixtieth year on the planet and have them ready to publish as the clock strikes midnight on the occasion of my 60th birthday: October 31, 2019. Sixty Songs at Sixty.

And so, here they are—a relatively neat and orderly collection of song lyrics for your perusal. I have tried to stay true to the original version of each song though the temptation was sometimes strong to want to tweak and update certain lyrics during the compilation process. For the most part, I have let the record speak, so to speak. Although the lyrics gathered here stand alone, without accompanying melodies, I hope you will find music in the words as you visit this collection.

Contents

POLISHING STONE — 1

Polishing Stone	2
All the Ways I Do	3
Here We Have Time	4
Waving Fields of August	5
Love So Big	6
Life is Short	7
Simple as it Seems	8
Full Moon	9
Fifty Times Around	10
The Thank You Song	11

ANOTHER YEAR OF SONG — 12

The Travelling	13
Fly Away	14
Pushing Through	15
This Shelter	16
Another Year of Song	17
Dreamtune	18
Broken Together	19

WHAT'S THE BIG IDEA?!? — 21

What's the Big Idea?!?	22
Who Loves You?!?	23
It's Not Easy Being a Kid	25
At the Drive Thru	27
Don't Wait Until Tomorrow	29
Wind-Up Parent	30
I'm Taking the Train	32
The Very Next Day	34
True Friend	35

ANYTHING IS POSSIBLE — 36

What if Kids Could Vote	37
The Reading Song	39
The 'Cat Woods' School Song	40

The First Avenue-Frontenac Song	41
Who is Molly Brant?	42
Anything is Possible!	43
Living on Wolfe Island	44
We're 100 Kids!	45
Wheels on the Bus	46
The Happy Sad Song	47
The Stuff Song	48
Who in the World?	49
Everyone Has A Bucket	50

HALFWAY ROUND THE WORLD 51

Halfway Round the World Waltz	52
Curving for the Coast, Part 1	53
Curving for the Coast, Part 2	55
Wrong Way Go Back	56
Lifeline	57
Painted Yellow: An Old-Time Tale	58
Black-letter Stammer	60

LEFT TO OUR OWN DEVICES 62

Postcard Town	63
Another Song	64
Courage to Spare	65
On My Way to Your House	66
The Dark Road Loves the Lover	67
Waiting for the Next Best Thing to Come Around	68
Metal Train	69
Gasoline, Guitars, Groceries & Guns	70
Emily & Eric (Late Night Amsterdam)	71
Ça me Fait Penser (It Makes Me Think)	72
Sticks & Stones	73
Left to Our Own Devices	74
Song for Norah Jones	75
Patron Saint	76

Polishing Stone

Polishing Stone

Went to the river — my heart on my sleeve
Looking for something to help me believe
The river is motion the currents run deep
Went to the river — polishing stone

Went to the mountains high as the sky
Feeling so small and wondering why
The forest was silent I was never alone
Went to the mountains — polishing stone

Polishing stone
Polishing stone
Going away and then coming home
Polishing stone
Polishing stone

Went to the highway — show me a sign
Wide like the ocean a thin white line
Feeling big love for these friends of mine
Went to the highway — polishing stone

The river is motion the currents run deep
It carves out this valley ancient and steep
Life is a promise I know I will keep
The river is motion — polishing stone

All the Ways I Do

See you sitting by your window
Guess you're wondering where the time goes
Fast and slow
To and fro
Out the gate and down the road

Try to count the ways I love you
It's like counting stars above you
Sparkle bright
First star tonight
Wish I may — wish I might

Tell you all the ways I do
Tell you every day I do
Through and through you know it's true
All the ways I do

Now we all know just how time flies
Sunset swings around to sunrise
Orange and pink
It makes you think
Miss the moment if you blink

So count your blessings — count on me
Set the table — pour some tea
I sing this love song just for you
For all the ways I do
For all the ways I do

See you sitting by your window …

Here We Have Time

We must learn to give to others
The things that we ourselves most need
A smile, a laugh, a kind word to offer
Love grows from the tiniest seed

And here is a song—a song for our children
All holding hands stretched out in a line
And here's to the love and life we are building
A love that is yours—a love that is mine

All of our children—so beautifully fine
They arrive and we greet them: Here we have time

And the music is yours
And the music is mine
And the music is love
Here we have time

A soft light falls coming in through the windows
Colours splash and dance on the floor
Love is the song the children all sing to
Music in waves touching the shore

Here is a place that's quiet and giving
With patience and kindness and love to spare
Open the doors and open the windows
Into the light—I'll meet you there

All of our children—so beautifully fine
They arrive and we greet them: Here we have time

And the story is yours
And the story is mine
And the story is love
Here we have time

Waving Fields of August

Children sleep the muse it hovers
Waving fields of August pass
Sweet wind tugs the golden covers
Remember this it may not last

Remember this it may not last
The future sweeps away the past
The future sweeps away the past
Remember this it may not last

Strangers pry your heart wide open
Though talismans are kept for fear
Travel leaves you full of hoping
Found-love disguised as souvenirs

Found-love disguised as souvenirs
A music box with rusted gears
A feeling you had but lost for years
Found-love disguised as souvenirs

It's a late summer highway
It's a late afternoon
It's late to be singing a late August tune
But I sing it now just for you two
Asleep in the back seat I sing it for you

So remember this it will live on
We sing our lifetimes into song
Life is short the days are long
Remember this it will live on

Love So Big

How do I do it when there's so much to it
So much love that I'm swimming through it
How do I show it when it's so clear I know it
So much love from this Sunday evening poet

How do I say it find the notes that might play it
Find a little song and a breeze that might sway it
How do I do it when there's so much to it
How do I give you this love?

A love so big and me so small
Summer ends and then comes Fall

This love I feel for everyone
The morning sky the setting sun
This love I feel for everyone
The day begins the day is done

So that's how I do it — guess there wasn't much to it
Opened my heart and let the love pass through it
That's how I do it yes that's how I do it
That's how I give you this love

And though each of you are scattered
It's only love that really matters
So I give you all this love
I give you all this love

Each and every one of you
A love that's old — a love that's new
I give you all of this love
I give you all of my love

Life is Short

Life is short so go real slow
Life is short and don't you know
You can try to hold time keep it close to your heart
Try to paint every dream that you dreamed from the start
But the colours will bleed and the images run
Leave you holding your breath chasing after the sun
Life is short so go real slow

What matters most is open to persuasion
What matter most is up for debate
What matters most comes down to the occasion
What matters most lives between faith and fate

So go real slow — go the way you've been wanting to go
You never know — fast may not be better than slow
Fast may not be better than slow

But what would I know about going slow?
What would I know about slow?
Fast Fast Fast that's the speed I go
There's a lot that I don't know about slow
There's a lot about slow that I don't know

Life is short so go real slow
Life is short and don't you know
That the colours fly by but they swing round again
So try to forget to keep remembering
Let go of time and stay close to your heart
Let the days come together let the days come apart

Life is short so go real slow
Life is short so go real slow
Life is short …

Simple as it Seems

Sometimes it's as simple as it seems
We are made for love — we are made for love
The heart knows exactly what it means
Cuz it's made for love — yes it's made for love

So you keep your heart as open as you can
Let love be your art it's a feeling not a plan
And you find your heart will travel to a place it's never been
Like a lost thread it unravels into gold and blue and green

Let the pain and fear move through you
Let the love and light undo you
Cuz the heart is made for love

Sometimes it's not as simple as it seems
We're afraid of love — we're afraid of love
The heart don't know exactly what it means
It's still made for love — it's still made for love

Yet you close your heart — you don't want to feel the pain
Can't bear to fall apart from the feelings you can't name
And sometimes we don't listen to what the heart has in mind
It's easy to lose courage and the heart is hard to find

Let the pain and fear move through you
Let the love and light undo you
Cuz the heart is made for love

Let the pain and fear move through you
Let the love and light undo you
Cuz the heart is made for love
Yes, the heart is made for love

Full Moon

The moon paints a picture outside my door
And scatters its shadows out across my floor
Light spills through windows and splashes on the wall
The night it is so quiet it's hardly there at all

The landscape becomes flooded with a delicate glow
The mountains stand so silent — all silhouettes and snow
The dark trees stretch upward expecting to fly
The stars are cast as witnesses to an unending sky

It's like looking out the window to find out where you are
Then you see your own reflection
You don't have to look that far
It's like looking at people to find out who you are
Then you look inside yourself

Sometimes I get to thinking until I can't think anymore
The times I win the times I lose the times I don't keep score
But now I'm taken back to places and the things that have since past
The times are meant to pass us by — the dreams are made to last
And I try to put some meaning to the patterns that I see
Somehow it feels like endless reels of film inside of me

It's like looking out the window to find out where you are
Then you see your own reflection
You don't have to look that far
It's like looking at people to find out who you are
Then you look inside yourself

The moon paints a picture outside of my door
And scatters its shadows out across my floor
Light spills through windows and splashes on the wall
The night it is so quiet it's hardly there at all
The moon paints a picture — full moon

Fifty Times Around

Fifty times around the sun
Some for pain some for fun
Fifty times and still not done
Fifty times around

Fifty times around the sun
I have so much while some have none
Thy Kingdom come Thy Will be done
Fifty times around

Fifty times around   Fifty times around

Fifty times around the moon
Whose shadow sings a different tune
Sometime late and sometime soon
The lost will join the found

Yes I have a family
I care for them they care for me
They teach me just how love can be
Every time around

Every time around   Every time around

Do you wonder how your life might go?
The years so fast the days so slow
So you send a prayer to heaven knows
For every time around

As you watch the day turn into night
The first star tumbles into sight
You love this life with all your might
Every time around

Every time around. In this life we've found. Every time around

And me I'm sixty times around the sun
Sixty times and still not done
Of the lucky souls I am one — every time around

The Thank You Song

The end has come to our day
There's one more thing I'd like to say
You've made it such a special day: thank you

With all of you I want to be
You're my secret recipe
Me and you and you and me: thank you

Thank you Thank you Thank you

Your laughter makes me feel so good
I ring the bell I knock on wood
I'd take you all home if I could

I sing this song with open heart
You teach me how to play my part
The end is really just a start: thank you

Let's celebrate this time we had
Lots of happy not much sad
So our goodbye won't feel so bad

There's one last thing I want to do
Before I say goodbye to you
There's one last thing I want to do:
Thank you Thank you Thank you

Another Year of Song

The Travelling

So we give ourselves to motion as the night rewrites the day
The wheels they speak of travel and the turning falls away
The road becomes the evening it bears witness to the song
Distance written on the body — the kind that makes us strong

Love will pull the stars around
Love to love this place we've found
Love the love that gathers here
The night sky whispers in our ear

Words are wings and words are ties
Words may never recognize
But words sail through this pale night sky
Through a tiny planet's eye
Lost is just a feeling but lost is also found
Lost is just a listening — a gathering of sound

Love will pull the stars around
Love to love this place we've found
Love the love that gathers here
The night sky whispers in our ear

Feel the headlights on the hill tonight
Coming down like moons
Through a forest filled with whispersong
A chorus filled with June

So we give up all our stories that don't remember flight
And laugh as all our worried words sail off out of sight
Bring the nighttime forward so that we might take our place
And listen for the listening — the hillside whispers grace

Love will pull the stars around …

Lyrics: GW Rasberry
Music: James Campbell, GW Rasberry, Rob Unger

Fly Away

I'm staring out the window — lost inside my room
Doesn't take too much to know — change is coming soon
Grey mountain tops scratch against the sky
Wind comes rushing in — breathes a heavy sigh

Battered leaves lay fallen all around
Like a worn out ship with its hull all run aground
And I wanna fly away

The clouds are thick — they hold no love today
They press in close — their tense mood on display
And tired out tufts of grass strain to keep their place
A slowly dying grip — a victim of their age

November rain falls harshly on the ground
The distant sun is nowhere to be found
And I wanna fly away

I'm trying to do the best that I can
I'm trying to do the best that I can
I'm trying to be the person — the person that I am
I'm trying to do the best that I can

But the spark that's in me is not here today
I hope it comes back soon — there's just no way to say
Cuz the fire that fuels it has burned down to a glow
Can't explain the way I feel — I really just don't know

Battered leaves lay fallen all around
Like a worn out ship with its hull all run aground
And I wanna fly away

Pushing Through

They say you learn a lesson every day
I learned more than that when I went away
I flew away — I was on the run
Heading out for the midnight sun
Searching for the person I might be
But you can never fly away far enough
Worrying about the smooth or tough
Life's an ocean — it can still get rough

Please come inside these words I sing for you
Take harbour in the light that's shining through
They say love can heal it can smooth the soul
Or lighten dark parts where you're afraid to go
So open up to who you really are
And take the course you trust inside
Ride it like an ocean tide
After all you know you've come this far

And the fear we feel from day to day as we shed our skin
So near so real and it's ok cuz it comes from within

Now I'm coming home mountains tearing at my heart
So much beauty here you know it may come apart
I'm seeing orange exploding out of green
And brilliant splashes of in-between
The leaves the trees the sky on this Fall day
So hey my friends just let me say
I've been at home and I've been away
I felt myself changing everyday — I was pushing through

Everybody gets tossed around it's the ocean of our lives
We're sometimes lost — we're sometimes found
It's a two-edged knife

So put your heart in every day
And say the things you want to say
Because realness never goes away
And there may not be another day
For pushing through

This Shelter

I don't want to live inside this shelter no more
It's time to come out and find out what life is for
Too easy to hide away and wait for another day
I don't want to live inside this shelter

The pressure of life gets bigger all the time
And everyone stares at you if your words don't rhyme
But you've got to live with yourself
So don't live it stuck on some shelf
The pressure of life gets bigger

I hope the sun shines on you today
I hope something good might come your way
I hope that love is here to stay

So who am I to tell you how to feel?
And who is to say that my words are for real
It's a simple message to share — if only to say that I care
So here I am just singing

I hope the sun shines on you today
I hope something good might come your way
I hope that love is here to stay

I don't want to live inside this shelter no more

Another Year of Song

Jump in my canoe — I'm coming out to see you — I'm rolling
Jump in my canoe — the sky is in full blue — I'm rolling

The forest pulls — you slide from shore
You wave as if there's something more
The surface holds you in its sway
The kind of blue that makes the day come rolling

Jump in my canoe — I'm coming out to see you — I'm rolling
Jump in my canoe — there's mist & rock cliffs too — I'm rolling

You write it down or else it's gone
You write it down you build a song
Cuz if you don't you'll never know
That this is how your lifeline flows — you're rolling

How many years? Back to back
Some like this and some like that
How many years? Just like that
A glacier bed — a welcome mat
The places where the Buddha sat

Jump in my canoe — I'm coming out to see you — I'm rolling
This may be nothing new but the day is up to you — you're rolling

Coming back again you bet we will be back again
Coming back again you bet we will be back again

Coming back again — so much more to say
The road that curves 'round Thunder Bay
Coming back again — the curve the flat
Another song carried on His back
A borrowed tune says 'thanks for that'

Jump in my canoe — I'm coming out to see you — I'm rolling
Jump in my canoe — coming out to see you …

Lyrics: GW Rasberry, with a nod to Ian Tamblyn — a Canadian treasure.
Music: James Campbell, GW Rasberry, Rob Unger

Dreamtune

Dreaming — dreaming it's our turn to go
Dreaming — the dream's dream rolling slow
Dreaming — of the crooked line that pulls us straight
Into dreaming — we drift toward the heron's gate

And the night grows deeper — deeper ...

Dreaming — of twenty mirrored lights that call
Dreaming — across the river down the hall
Dreaming — gather here with sixteen souls
Dreaming — blowing on the sacred coals

And the night grows deeper — deeper ...

Words that dance toward the fire
Wings that pull the sadness higher
Words that won't and words that will
Caught among the forestspill

Dreaming — a dark lake whispers
Dreaming — speaks to seven secret sisters
Dreaming — breathe among the few who know
Dreaming — as the stars begin to show

And the night grows deeper — deeper ...

Words that dance toward the fire
Wings that pull the sadness higher
Words that won't and words that will
Caught among the forestspill

Dreaming — pulling the day like a broken wagon
Dreaming — pulling the day like a broken wagon

Lyrics: GW Rasberry
Music: James Campbell, GW Rasberry, Rob Unger

Broken Together

Feels like we are broken — trying to restart
Part of us together — part of us apart

Feels like we are burning — a single roadside flare
The dark is light that's turning — a flame in search of air

Stay between the lines — turning on a dime
Maybe not this time: this time broken

Feels like we are broken — trying to repair
Words we have not spoken — riding with no spare

Read between the lines — keeper of the signs
Guess how many times: this time broken

Love comes so unpolished
Love is unaware
Love is and isn't working
Love is and isn't fair

You've got to love love when it's working
And when love isn't there
You've got to love love when it's working
And when love isn't …

And the good news is the bad news
And the bad news isn't good
One missed understanding — two misunderstood

But the good news isn't bad news
And the bad news can be good
The hurt that we can move beyond
Is the work we've understood

As our work — as love's work — as work that love requires
As love's work — as our work — love's work to tend the fires

Feels like we are moving on into the night
Shadow and forgiveness — love at second sight
Love stretched out in time — the road is curved and fine
A prayer two souls might find to keep love open

Lyrics: GW Rasberry
Music: James Campbell, GW Rasberry, Rob Unger

What's the Big Idea?!?

What's the Big Idea?!?

What's the big idea?!?
What's the big idea?!?
What's the big idea?!?

The big idea is big for sure
It's organically ground it's totally pure
It's guaranteed to hold the cure — it's a big idea for sure
It's a big idea for sure

The big idea won't save us time — it might be sad it might be fine
It's a polka-dotted valentine
It's a big idea for sure — it's a big idea for sure

What's the big idea?!?
What's the big idea?!?
What's the big idea?!?

The big idea is sometimes funny — it's partly cloudy it's partly sunny
It's a cup of tea served with honey
It's a big idea for sure

The big idea — I'm thinking of
The big idea — it fits like a glove
The big idea — all you need is …

Love each day the way it comes
Love your Dad — Love your Mom
Brothers sisters — neighbours, too
Give your love save some for you
And love the big idea!

Love the big idea!

Lyrics: GW Rasberry
Music: David Archibald

Who Loves You?!?

Who loves you? Who loves you? Who loves you?
Your dog & your cat do
Who loves you? Who loves you? Who loves you?
Your dog & your cat do
Plus a gold fish and a hamster too
That's who loves you
That's who — that's who — that's who loves you

Who loves you? Who loves you? Who loves you?
Your Mom & your Dad do
Who loves you? Who loves you? Who loves you?
Your Mom & your Dad do
Plus your Grandma & a best friend too
That's who loves you
That's who — that's who — that's who loves you

Raise your hands if you love you
Cuz you know it's up to you
Raise your hands to show it's true
Then we'll know for sure — simple, sweet and pure
Just who loves you. You do! You do! You do love you

Do you? Do you? Do you ? Do you?
Do you? Do you? Do you? Do you?
Do you? Do you? Do you love you?
I hope you do — I hope you do — I really really really do
I hope — hope you love you
I hope you do I — I hope you do — I really really really do
I hope — hope you love you

Who else loves you? Who else loves you?

Uncle Chris and your best friend June
Who moved last year to Saskatoon
Grandpa Dave and your cousin Jill
The Jackson family up the hill
Noah Sophie Jenny & Pete
Bob the dog who lives across the street
Your stuffed giraffe named Mister Q
Sarah, Scott and Jennifer too

Aunt Phyllis who always pulls your leg
Your cousins who live in Winnipeg
All these people who hold you dear
In case you forgot I'm telling you here

You give your love & you get some too
You love yourself & your Self loves you

That's who loves you
That's who — that's who — that's who loves you!

It's Not Easy Being a Kid

It's not easy being a kid
Everybody telling you not to do what they did
Everybody telling you not to do what they did
It's not easy being a kid

My Dad said when he was a kid he did some bad stuff
Stole some gum lied to his mom and acted real tough
Broke some rules stole some tools set fire to the shed
Thought he'd be cool around the school got grounded instead

Don't do what he did — don't do what he did
Don't get in all that trouble — don't do what he did

My Aunt said, "I should be dead!" when she fell from that tree
She climbed too high and poked her eye — got stung by a bee
It was almost dark when she reached the park and started to climb
She knew all along she was doing wrong but she didn't mind

Don't do what she did — don't do what she did
Don't get in all that trouble — don't do what she did

But how are we supposed to learn?!
It's only fair we get our turn
To get into trouble of our own — with our friends or all alone
We want to get in trouble too — we really really really do
To know what's right but do what's wrong
And worry our parents all night long

My Mom told me she took the car when she was 15
She didn't have her license if you know what I mean
Quick as a mouse snuck out of house and drove to the store
Didn't get very far cuz she smashed the car into the front door

Don't do what she did — don't do what she did
Don't get in all that trouble — don't do what she did

My Brother told me a story from his earlier days
He was only 8 when he climbed the gate and wandered away
Our parents thought he was sleeping all snug in his bed
But he was watching TV at the neighbours instead

Don't do what he did — don't do what he did
Don't get in all that trouble — don't get in all that trouble

Don't do what he did
Don't do what she did
Don't do what they did
Don't do what we did!

At the Drive Thru

In the backseat with my Sister at the Drive Thru
At the Drive Thru — At the Drive Thru
My Mom my Dad my Brother and the dog, too
And the lineup is 12 cars long

I'm hoping for some French fries at the Drive Thru
At the Drive Thru — At the Drive Thru
A burger and hot chocolate and some ice cream, too
And the lineup is 11 cars long

This could be a bad day if my Mother doesn't get her latté
Makes it feel just like a Monday on a Saturday afternoon

Don't mean to be complaining at the Drive Thru
At Drive Thru — At the Drive Thru
But this whole thing feels insane here at the Drive Thru
And the lineup is 10 cars long

Sometimes I wonder why no one's inside
Empty tables Empty chairs
It looks clean and cozy but no one is there

Cuz everybody's lined up at the Drive Thru
At the Drive Thru — At the Drive Thru
Doesn't make a lot of sense to me now how about you?
And the lineup is 9 cars long

9 cars long. 9 cars long. See how we wait. See how we wait

Our dog is getting restless at the Drive Thru
At the Drive Thru — At the Drive Thru
He's chewing on the arm-rest and the seat belt, too
And the lineup is 8 cars long

Last time he ate two dozen donuts and some chili, too
And some chili too at the Drive Thru
That's why he's so excited wouldn't you be too?
And the lineup is 7 cars long

This could be a good day now that we're only 6 cars away
Hey Look! Now we're only 5 cars away
Everything's going to be ok

I'm fighting with my Sister at the Drive Thru
At the Drive Thru — At the Drive Thru
Threw an orange peel but I missed her at the Drive Thru
And the lineup is 4 cars long

Sometimes I wonder why no one's inside
Empty tables Empty chairs
It looks clean and cozy but no one is there

My Dad is getting angry at the Drive Thru
At the Drive Thru — At the Drive Thru
He's mad at me, He's mad at her, He's mad at you
And the lineup is 3 cars long

3 cars long. 3 cars long
See how we wait. See how we wait
We put in our orders we're waiting our turn
Reaching the window's our only concern
You'd think that by now maybe we might have learned
3 cars long. 3 cars long.

Seagulls fighting over bagels at the Drive Thru
At the Drive Thru — At the Drive Thru
Racoons on picnic tables at the Drive Thru
And the lineup is 2 cars long

Our dog is throwing up now at the Drive Thru
At the Drive Thru — At the Drive Thru
The whole car's going crazy at the Drive Thru
But at least we're first in line
Cuz we've been waiting all this time
We're at the window — and we're first in line!

Co-written with Dave Clark

Don't Wait Until Tomorrow

Don't wait until tomorrow — don't wait until next week
Don't wait until the perfect time — to take a little peek
Don't wait another moment — don't wait another day
Just wait until your Dad gets home
That's what your Mom might say!

Don't wait until the rain stops — before you start to play
Don't wait until you're really sure — that everything's ok
Don't wait until tomorrow — if you're sure today
Just wait until your Mom gets home
That's what your Dad might say!

Why wait friends?   When you could do it now
Why wait friends? Don't need to show you how
Why wait friends? When you could do it now
Down the stairs through the gate with a cartwheel and a bow!

Don't wait until the sun shines — to live a sunny life
Don't wait until you've used a fork — before you use a knife
Don't wait until you're really sure — that the time is right
Don't wait until the holidays — to stay up late at night

Don't wait until it's perfect — every single time
Don't wait until you've used all yours — before you ask for mine
Don't wait until you're ready — to try it by yourself
Don't wait until you're taller — to reach the highest shelf

Why wait friends? It's time to show some style
Why wait friends? You've been doing it all the while
Why wait friends? To show us your great smile
Shed a tear, laugh out loud and do it all in style!

If a cloud comes sailing by don't worry your mind
Don't let it rain on your parade — let's have a good time
Let's sing a song all day long — let's dance in the breeze
Let's run and laugh in the waving grass and beautiful trees

Don't wait until tomorrow. Don't wait until tomorrow

Co-written with Dave Clark

Wind-Up Parent

What if you wind up a parent — what are you going to see?
An adult moving ever so swiftly — after you've wound up the key
What if you wind up a parent and just keep on turning the key?
Crank it too far and there you are with too much responsibility

Running after toddlers running late for school
Shivering with your daughter in the community pool
Baby Beluga is your favourite song
You find yourself singing it all day long

Of the 500 things you were hoping to do
Now you're life has come down to discussions of poo
Poo in the diaper — poo on the floor
There's no poo in the toilet but that's what toilet training's for
Breast feeding tips you share on your blog
You drink one more coffee to clear out the fog ...

And you're wound up — wound up
Drinking red wine out of sippy cups
Your baby won't nap and your toddler won't settle
For all this work you should be getting a medal
Pile up the dishes mop up the floor
Do a load of laundry — run to the store
Changing diapers all day long
Grab another coffee — please make it real strong
You're reading a story now you're singing a song
Hoping on hope that nothing goes wrong

Cuz you're wound up — wound up
Someone started turning the sound up
Breast-feeding mama trying not to go sour
Wake up to feed 'em every other hour
You're tired so tired it's the middle of the night
Your skin's feeling loose and your clothes are feeling tight
Despite it all — despite everything
You wouldn't want to change a single thing

What if you wind up a parent — who are you going to be?
Loving a child with all of your heart — unconditionally
You didn't know you could love quite this big
24/7 — it's the parenting gig
Your life feels so crazy — your life feels so good
Running on love and knocking on wood

So now that you've wound up a parent —
Your life measured by moments of grace
A crooked grin a teething ring wouldn't change a thing
For that look on your sleeping child's face …

Now you've wound yourself into a wind-up parent
Can't cover it up cuz it's so transparent
You love the crazy beautiful life that you live
Love the crazy beautiful gifts you can give
You're so darn happy it makes you weep
You just wish you had a little more sleep

Now they're all grown up but it doesn't seem easier
Tuition fees climbing and it makes you queasier
Your kids talking 'bout kids of their own
Gonna buy a little house with a great big loan

You're still a parent but it's never too late
And the good news is you graduate
Can't remember all the parenting stuff that you did
All that parenting stuff that you did
And now you're gonna have — Grandkids!

I'm Taking the Train

I'm taking the train — cuz my car uses too much gas
I'm taking the train — cuz the plane just goes too darn fast
I'm taking the train — steady humming on silver wheels
I'm taking the train — cuz I love how this country feels
Yes, I love how this country feels

Gonna set our sails — Gonna ride the silver rails
Gonna set our sails — Gonna ride the silver rails
Gonna ride the silver rails

You take your ticket and go — East or West let your heart decide
Sometimes you don't know — you're just in for a good long ride
I'm taking the train — it's like a village that moves on wheels
I'm taking the train — cuz I love how this country feels
Yes, I love how this country feels

Looking out the window — scene after scene
Passing through towns that call out to me
Field after field — tree after tree
Feeling like part of history

Gonna set our sails — Gonna ride the silver rails
Gonna set our sails — Gonna ride the silver rails
Gonna ride the silver rails

Gonna start with me and you — Then we'll make a friend or two
Gonna start with me and you — Then we'll make a friend or two

There's a country here to see — And the train's the place to be
There's a country here to see — And the train's the place to be

I'm taking the train—cuz my car uses too much gas
I'm taking the train—cuz the plane just goes too darn fast
I'm taking the train—steady humming on silver wheels
I'm taking the train—cuz I love how this country feels

Yes, I love how this country feels

The Very Next Day

You may have heard the story of the Cat Came Back
About a feral feline who lived out in a shack
He seemed to live a quiet life basking in the sun
Little did he know that his life had just begun

He had dreams of being on the stage loving every gig
Sure enough as time went by the Cat would make it big
Then he became reclusive very little would he say
Rumour had it he'd come back the very next day

The Very Next Day — The Very Next Day
We heard it might happen — The Very Next Day

So, they threw a great big party — you know what I mean
Animals of every shape and size would make the scene
Like a movie or a musical playing on Broadway
There was meowing, barking, howling from pedigree to stray

The Cat Came Back — the rumours were all true
He slid out of the limo grinning right on cue
Glowing like a Persian Prince whiskers to his toes
He wore a white tuxedo with a single red rose

Suddenly a cloud of smoke — a brilliant flash of light
The Cat simply disappeared — vanished in the night
Maybe this is what he planned his whole life long
His name is now a legend every time we sing the song

The Very Next Day — The Very Next Day
We heard it might happen — The Very Next Day

Fred was there at the beginning — of that you can be sure
Now the song and the story forever will endure
Every single one of us can make a dream come true
The Cat will keep on coming back — coming back to you

Co-written with Fred Penner and Rae Ellen Bodie

True Friend

With a true, true friend — a true, true friend
With a hand to hold or a hand to lend
And If you are lucky and I hope that you are
Your true, true friend loves you just as you are

Having a friend is a beautiful thing
It's like having a beautiful song to sing
And having a beautiful song to sing
Is like having a friend and that's a beautiful thing

With a true, true friend — a true, true friend
With a hand to hold or a hand to lend
And if you are lucky and I hope that you are
Your true, true friend loves you just as you are

Having a friend is like singing a song
You find out that others are singing along
And everything's right and nothing is wrong
You find yourself singing all day long

Friendship's old fashioned — it's new fangled too
You can visit an old friend out of the blue
You can Facebook or Skype or send a text too
Friendship's old fashioned and it's new fangled too

With a true, true friend — a true, true friend
With a hand to hold or a hand to lend
And if you are lucky and I hope that you are
Your true, true friend loves you just as you are

Yes, if you are lucky and I know that you are
Your true, true friend loves you just as you are

Anything is Possible

What if Kids Could Vote

What if kids could vote? All around the world
Every boy and every girl — All around the world
All around the world

What if kids could vote? Starting today
What if kids could vote and truly have their say?
If we asked them to tell us how they really feel
If we asked them to tell us what is really real

How our world would start to change
If we let the children rearrange
All of the rules that we have put in place
For all of the ways we run the human race

What if kids could vote? All around the world
World leaders please take note — All around the world
All around the world

There'd be nobody living on the street
Everybody gets enough to eat
You can feel the feeling all around the world

It's time to rewrite history with a future free of poverty
You can feel the feeling all around the world

Imagine all the people — that's what John would say
Imagine all the people living for today
All around the world

For a hope that lights our days and nights
For a world that honours human rights
You can feel the feeling all around the world

Everybody gets to feel some love
The sea below the stars above
No more hate and no more fear
The whole thing becomes crystal clear
You can feel the feeling all around the world

Everybody has a voice — Everybody has a choice
You can feel the feeling all around the world

What if kids could vote? All around the world
World leaders please take note — All around the world
Grab your hat and grab your coat! — All around the world

All around the world

The Reading Song

We're all singing the Reading Song
The Reading Song — The Reading Song
Reading aloud — Singing along
Singing the Reading Song

I love to read — You love to read
He loves to read — She loves to read
One day someone just planted a seed
Now we all love to read

And it's not just a matter of love
But also a matter of need
When push comes to shove — we do what we love
Now we all need to read. That's why …

We're all singing the Reading Song
The Reading Song — The Reading Song
Reading aloud — Singing along
Singing the Reading Song

We Do. We can. We will and we must
In paperback and hardcover we trust
We Do. We can. We will and we must
On the train the plane the boat or the bus
Indeed — we all need to read
Indeed — we all need to read

We're all singing the Reading Song
The Reading Song — The Reading Song
Reading aloud — Singing along
Singing the Reading Song

Reading aloud — Singing along
Singing the Reading Song
Singing aloud — Reading along
Singing the Reading Song

The 'Cat Woods' School Song
For Cataraqui Woods School

Cat Woods! Cat Woods! Cataraqui Woods!
Our school's got. Our school's got — the Cataraqui goods!

Cat Woods school includes everybody
As we work and we play and as we study
That's the way it's done
There's room for everyone

I can be me and you can be you
Even if we have different points of view
Each of us plays our part
We're Cataraqui Smart

Cataraqui — Green and blue
Cataraqui — Me and you
Cataraqui Woods

When it's time to play — count us in
Let the Cataraqui fun begin
It's a Science and an Art
To be Cataraqui Smart

When there's work to be done — we do it
It's not easy but we stick to it
We finish what we start
We're Cataraqui Smart

Our differences all come together
Through sunny skies and stormy weather
We play it from the heart
We're Cataraqui Smart

Cataraqui — Walks the walk
Cataraqui — Talks the talk
Cataraqui — We Rock!

Cat Woods! Cat Woods! Cataraqui Woods!
Our school's got. Our school's got — the Cataraqui goods!

The First Avenue-Frontenac Song

Our school is Frontenac — You're First Avenue
Your school is First Avenue — We are Frontenac

Our school's going to be your school
And your school's going to be our school

My school — Your school — Our school — How cool!
That's how it will be — at Molly Brant Elementary

Frontenac — First Avenue
A little bit of me — A little bit of you
First Avenue — Frontenac
Together there's no looking back

We'll keep the best of the old and mix it with the new
Just think of all the new things our new school will be
At Molly Brant Elementary

Yes, our school's going to be your school
And your school's going to be our school

My school — Your school — Our school — How cool!
That's how it will be — at Molly Brant Elementary
At Molly Brant Elementary

To commemorate the merging of Frontenac Elementary School and First Avenue School to form Molly Brant Elementary School

Who is Molly Brant?
For Simon Pottery's Class at Molly Brant Elementary School

Who was Molly Brant? Who was Molly Brant?
Who was Molly Brant? It's so hard to know
Almost 300 years — it was so long ago

It was so long ago — back through history we go
Our past is a story — like a river it flows
It was so long ago but not so far away
She lived on the shore where we're standing today

Who was Molly Brant? Who was Molly Brant?

She was a Mohawk woman we remember today
For the part in history that Molly Brant played
And history tells a story we'll try to understand
A history that is built on Indigenous land

Who is Molly Brant? Who is Molly Brant?
Who is Molly Brant? She is part of our school
Who is Molly Brant? She is part of our school

She is part of our story — she is part of our past
She is part of our future — and her name it will last

We are Molly Brant — We are Molly Brant
We are Molly Brant — We are part of this school
We are Molly Brant — We are part of this school
We are Molly Brant

Anything is Possible!
For Molly Brant Elementary School

Anything is possible—anything at all
If I believe and you believe then we can do it all

Anything is possible—just you wait and see
Anything is possible—it starts with you and me

Right here! Right now!
We will show you—show you how
Right here! Right now!
We will show you—show you how

Someone says, "Impossible!"
Someone shouts, "No Way!"
Someone else is full of doubt every single day
But we can make a window where there used to be a wall
Anything is possible—anything at all

Anything at all
We are ten feet tall
Anything at all
We are ten feet tall

Anything is possible—just you wait and see
Anything is possible—it starts with you and me
Anything is possible—just you wait and see
Anything is possible …

Living on Wolfe Island

For Marysville Public School

Wind & Water — Sun & Sky
Ice in December — Waves in July
Wind & Water — Sun & Sky
These are all the reasons why

We're singing and we're smiling
Cuz we're living on Wolfe Island
The island is the place we call our home
The island is a place we call our own

You can see Kingston across the way
The ferry goes back and forth all day
Back and forth — forth and back
It takes you away but it brings you back

Where the St. Lawrence River meets the lake
There's a 1000 islands give or take
Green on blue — blue on green
It's a beautiful watercolour scene

Wind & Water — Sun & Sky
Ice in December — Waves in July
Wind & Water — Sun & Sky
These are all the reasons why

We're singing and we're smiling
Cuz we're living on Wolfe Island
The island is the place we call our home
The island is a place we call our own

We're 100 Kids!
For 100 Kids Kingston

We're 100 Kids!
We're 100 strong!
We're writing a new story
We're singing a new song

We're 100 Kids!
We're 100 strong!
We hope that you will join us
We hope you'll come along

We're 100 Kids who really, really care
We're just like other kids living everywhere
But we have more than others — yes we have more than most
And we have many gifts to share so we propose a toast

We give to you our talents — our treasures and our time
We hope to make a better life — we hope to really shine

We want to make a difference
We want to rearrange
The ways we all might share the world
We want to make a change

We're 100 Kids!
We're 100 strong!
We're writing a new story
We're singing you this song

Wheels on the Bus
For Kingston Transit Artist "Pop-up" Event

The driver on the bus she is driving
Down the street you're standing on
She only stops for a moment — lets you in and then she's gone
She's driving right on cue
She's driving just for you — and you and you and you

Does the driver dream she's sailing over oceans big and blue?
Or does she dream she's driving a BMW?
She's driving right on cue
She's driving just for you — and you and you and you

And the wheels on the bus go round and round
The wheels on the bus go round and round
The wheels on the bus they go round and round
All through the town
The wheels go round and round

Do you hope you keep your balance?
Find your seat without falling down
Do you feel the people staring? Do you feel eyes all around?
The people in your town
All the sights and sounds
Can you feel it all around?

And the wheels on the bus go round and round
The wheels on the bus go round and round
The wheels on the bus they go round and round
All through the town
The wheels go round and round

Are you feeling like a stranger — are you feeling all alone?
Could you use a little love now?
Won't find it on your cell phone
So why not give a smile?
To the folks across the aisle?
Why not drive in style?

And the wheels on the bus go round and round ...

The Happy Sad Song

It's a happy sad song — It's a happy sad song
If you're hap-hap happy or sad you can sing along

I'm sad to see happy go
Happy's a friend I've been happy to know
But sad is here guess I'll go with the flow
Still I'm sad to see happy go

One minute happy — next one sad
A touch of good with a bit of bad
It's a bit confusing that's for sure
I'm still looking for the Happy-Sad cure

It's a happy sad song — It's a happy sad song
If you're hap-hap happy or sad you can sing along

Feelings come and feelings go
It's good to let your feelings show

Happy and sad — green and blue
Maybe you've had these feelings too
Sad and happy — blue and green
And all of the feelings in between

I'm sad to see happy go
Happy goes fast — sad goes slow
Feelings come and feelings go
Still I'm happy to see sad go

It's a happy sad song — It's a happy sad song
If you're hap-hap happy or sad you can sing along

The Stuff Song

We want more stuff!
We want more stuff!
We want stuff!

We need less stuff!
We need less stuff!
No more stuff!

Stuff Stuff Stuff Stuff Stuff Stuff Stuff
We need stuff!
Stuff Stuff Stuff Stuff Stuff Stuff Stuff
 No more stuff!

We need the upgrade
A new look a new shade
We like the old one
It still works — it's still fun

Let us all go shop now
Shop until we drop now
We want stuff

Let us stay at home now
Enjoy what we have now
No more stuff

More stuff is what we need
Maximum stuff at maximum speed
More stuff is what we need

Less cars more bicycles
Reduce reuse recyclable
More stuff we don't need

Always consuming
Business is booming
Shopping cart zooming

More or less stuff??

Who in the World?
For Mr. Caldwell's Class at Centennial Public School

Who in the world am I?
Who in the world are you?
We promise to always try
We promise to always do

The things that help us understand
Who you are and who I am
Together we can make a plan
To help us understand

Having a voice and speaking out
Discovering what this world's about
We laugh. We cry. We sing and shout
It's what this world's about

Who in the world are you?
Who in the world am I?
We promise to always do
We promise to always try

A voyage of discovery
Sometimes we may disagree
On how to solve a mystery
Together you and me

Who in the world am I?
Who in the world are you?
We promise to always try
We promise to always do

Who in the world are we?

Everyone Has A Bucket
For Mrs. Sirman's Class at Lancaster Elementary School

Everyone has a bucket
That's invisible to the eye
When it's full we feel happy
When it's empty we might cry

The key to being happy is in this choice we make
We will fill the bucket—never dip and never take

Share a toy
Give a smile
Invite a friend to play for a while

Use kind words all the time
Take turns and we'll all feel fine

Everyone has a bucket
That's invisible to the eye
When it's full we feel happy
When it's empty we might cry

The key to being happy is in this choice we make
We will fill the bucket—never dip and never take.

Based on the book, "Have you Filled a Bucket Today? A Guide to Daily Happiness for Kids" by Carol McCloud. Illustrated by David Messing.

Halfway Round the World

Halfway Round the World Waltz

I flew halfway around the world
I flew half the way round — halfway lost halfway found
Sang the song without making a sound
Halfway up to come halfway back down

I swam halfway around the world
Trying my best not to change — now isn't that strange?
How despite everything I've been shown
How a person will cling to what's known

Halfway around — going up and coming halfway around
Going up and coming halfway around

I stumbled halfway around the world
It was nothing at all — just a trip then a fall
But the landing felt good just the same
Another chance to remember my name

Halfway round the sea the sky the ground
And you will always be
Halfway round the sea the sky the ground
The waltz will set you free

And now I'm halfway around the world
It's not always a test — I just needed a rest
A little courage to help find my way
A wing a prayer and a borrowed cliché

And what I'm trying to say — in an unspoken way
Halfway old halfway young — another song just begun
With the sky upside down — the stars floating around
I'll take the true with the false and do the overseas waltz

And if you'll all be so kind — that is if no one would mind
Let's go half the way round 'till the world's upside down
And do the halfway around the world waltz
The halfway around the world waltz

Curving for the Coast, Part 1

You become a straight line — curving for the coast
Become a straight line curving — you've never been this close

And the light is why you're on this road
It's a weight yet has no load — there's no baggage to unload

Yes the light is who you are right here
On this road for love and fear — colour blind and crystal clear

Yellowy fields, tumbled out, tired and scattered. Scratch and scrub. Everything looking for a name, here. No name needed. Nothing needed. Still, the light. Still the light moves from the inside out but it's too soon to invoke Grace this early in the trip, it's just the light. It's just that everything it touches turns to …

The landscape run backwards now — a strange familiar scene
Shot through a projector — spooling green and green

Just a place between the ground and sky
Ours is not to question why — watch the colours as they fly

Like a voice you've heard but never seen
Like a water colour dream — a place you've never been

Papery grasses, held, waiting in windsway and the sun pouring itself out over everything. The soil: spectacular, rusted. And all the colours in and out of focus. In and out of focus. Unfamiliar forest bears witness: bark, frayed and hanging. Tinder dry. Eucalypt. Paper bark tea-tree, Spotted Gum, Grey Ironbark, tall Mallee scrub.

It's early but you're in for the long haul with tension enough to pull the unsuspecting. Tinder dry and then ferns. Ferns become fragile cover as you sudden-drop down into valley and shadow and then climb back up into parched abundance. Perfection enough to disorient with the line running out and out …

Right-hand drive, left-side leaning
Left to contemplate left over meaning
Right-hand drive, left-side leaning
Left to contemplate left over meaning

The Great Dividing Range
The familiar swallowed by the strange
The Great Dividing Range
The familiar swallowed by the strange
The Great Dividing Range: this world, that world
This world, that world
It's enough to pull the unsuspecting ...

Curving for the Coast, Part 2

There's colour coming through the trees from such a long way off
Colour coming through the trees — it's a hard blue painted soft

And the blue is why you're on this road
It's a blue that might explode — there's no language there's no code

And you're pulled toward this kind of blue
Like a spell you can't undo — for the many for the few

There's colour coming through the trees from such a long way off. The air gives itself away. And every ocean you've ever seen now conjured. Inlets and arms are the messengers that send word. There is nothing else this big. Colour coming through the trees. And the long descent. Don't even mention blue. The tides doing all the work. The sound blinds you to any other sense. And there it is. Look as far as you will. Cue the waves …

All the words you cannot speak are here: torn away, torn away. Rip tides, wind, cloud-chasing. The sand says, 'Walk Here,' as far as you are willing. Mystery Bay really isn't. Really is. There is nothing else this big. The towns will try to tell you otherwise. Rooms with views and any number of stars above the door. Contradictions abound. The world held upside down for the tourist with traveller's intention. Climate control and other oxymorons are poorly signed.

Roadways cling to the coast with an awkward sense of normalcy and go on and on toward forever — or at least Melbourne.

But not you, no, not you, not you. It's your First Trip. Your first little trip. Go on and stumble … feel the long stretch of humble because your loop is finite and tiny. The ocean will give way to mountains that shake themselves back out into scrub and outback without notice. Only a faded, 'Give Way,' sign nailed to a post to suggest otherwise.

It's your First Trip. Your first little trip and you are that small. Unwanted almost. The sun pouring itself out. And all the colours. The sun pouring itself out. And all the colours. The line running out and out. And all the colours …

Wrong Way Go Back

Large sign. Bright red
Miss it: You're dead

Red sign. Large print
Go back: You're first hint

Driving too fast. Driving too slow
No in-between. Nowhere to go

Driving too slow. Driving too fast
Driving right by. Driving right past

So you're over, down under — your head's out of whack
Over and under: Wrong Way Go Back

Freeway confusion — better pick up the slack
You're on the left side: Wrong Way Go Back

Now you're all caffeinated — smoked the whole pack
You're so over-rated: Wrong Way Go Back

Wrong Way Go Back. Wrong Way Go Back. Wrong Way Go Back

Bright sign. Dim wit
Short sight. Deep shit

One sign. Two eyes
Wrong way: Surprise

Driving too fast. Driving too slow
No in-between. Nowhere to go

Driving too slow. Driving too fast
Driving right by. Driving right past

Summertime and the driving ...
Concrete surfing — no time to be slack
Watch for the road kill — keep the Southern Cross at your back

Lifeline

Your horses don't fit your barn
Your tractor don't match your farm
Twice the work and half the charm: Hold your own

All the while your crops were thinning
Paper says the Blue Team's winning
Hard to keep your head from spinning: Hold your own

All this time gone
All this time gone: so long
Down a dirt road, the forty foot — it's like a twisting song

Your lifeline is in the field
You're crazy trying to farm The Shield
But picking rocks is part of the deal: Hold your own

All this time gone
All this time gone: so long
Halfway left and partly right — it's like a twisting song

You said you're never going to leave this farm — never
No, you're never going to leave this farm — never
No one's ever going to twist your arm — ever

The factory farm is hungry now
It's got an appetite that won't allow
Your life your land your own two hands
Or maybe a government with other plans

Your tractor don't fit your barn
Your horses don't match your farm
Second mortgage and a lucky charm: Hold your own

Lyrics: GW Rasberry
Music: James Campbell, GW Rasberry, Rob Unger

Painted Yellow: An Old-Time Tale

Scene 1, Late Summer Dream, Part 1

I'm thinking August. Late August. A still-awake-but-growing-tired August. Late, late summer: The Big Lull. Laneways lined with weeds that won't quit. Rural Ontario. Fields on fields on fields. And corn. Fields of corn. I'm driving, drifting, dreaming. Driving, drifting, dreaming. Thinking impossible thoughts of last March, April, May: those tiny seeds trying to remember what a whole field painted yellow smells like.

But now children float in butter-dipped dreams of water barrels that spell August in fields taller than the tallest kid in the whole school. Yes, recess is right around the corner of every mouth poised and every September lunch pail ever packed. Chores, chores and more chores. Chores, chores and more chores. And all the wiry old farmers smiling the machinery back into the drive shed. And why are they smiling? They're smiling because it hurts so much. (Anyone spoken with a farmer lately?)

Someone whispers, "frost" but laughter melts the thought of school bells and rubber boots and the summer still feels fatter than a big old moon. A harvest moon—the yellow face of fiction shining right through myth.

Scene 2, Harvest (The Big Gathering)

Butter and bad jokes —the same ones as last year
Butter and bad jokes —the same ones as last year
Dust. Crooked teeth. Paper plates. Dust. Crooked teeth.
Paper plates. [Ya, I know, paper plates. They're flimsy. They're pretty much useless but rituals are rituals.]

Butter and bad jokes —the same ones as last year
Butter and bad jokes —the same ones as last year
Dust. Crooked teeth. Paper plates. Dust. Crooked teeth.
Paper plates. Home-baked pies to follow. Home-baked
pies to follow.

Scene 3, Late Summer Dream, Part 2

The clouds drift without moving and green has painted the landscape so long now that white seems pretty much unthinkable (winter having not yet been invented). I grow these poems, well, I grow these poems because they're all I know how to grow (all farm hands having weathered storms much worse than poetry, mine or anyone else's). I grow these poems, call them songs, sometimes. Grow these poems, sometimes call them songs. And corn on the cob? Yes, corn on the cob always comes with such a sweet surprise ending, like old Jimmy Grayson who spends the whole summer sitting on the porch resting his eyelids only to pull out a tired old fiddle and dance summer backwards.

Nightfall: darkness starts a fire and nobody's thinking about corn stuck in their teeth or mortgages or wage-freezes with a campfire calling the tune ... never mind the key or the fancy chords. The dance floor's just a dirt patch anyhow. Go on. Cut the rug, Jimmy!

Scene 4, Poets, Farmers and Heavy Machinery

Still, I know I'll never fit in here with just my words to plant. (Hell, I've still got all my fingers.) So, I shove some words in the ground when the calendar reads 'May' and watch them grow in crazy rows all summer: tiny seeds trying to remember what a whole field painted yellow smells like. Tiny seeds trying to remember. Trying to remember. What a whole field painted yellow smells like.

Paint it yellow.
Painted yellow.

Black-letter Stammer

Black-letter stammer: for a 1948 Underwood typewriter that lives in the forest. Word machine. Black metal creature. Beautiful monster.

Twenty-two frogs are making love in the south swamp
I swear it's true. Yes, it's as true as a metaphor

For moonlight or black as the paddle's dip into midnight
Where there's no need for push or pull

Twenty-two frogs are making love, I swear, and the south
Swamp is a metaphor for directions   lost.

Twenty-two frogs. And the metaphor is love
Making itself known. Love making itself.

Love-making — where there's no need for metaphor
No need for moonlight. Love — where there's no need.

The words are songs and the songs are poems
And the poems are type-written. Type-written and

Dead afraid of these metal signposts that point
to where I am   not.
Type-written memos complete with cryptic
references and existential font.

Maybe to be lost first would suggest a way out instead
of worrying about where the keys are
on this heavy metal acoustic typewriter

Where the keys are type-written and dead afraid.
Dead afraid but never better off dead than afraid.

A confusion of night with sound
Otherwise the gift is completely realized.

A confusion of night with sound
Otherwise the gift is completely realized.

A confusion of night with sound
When metal strikes a chord to pattern the owl.

It's like a locomotive waking up the forest.
Metal-on-metal: a black-letter'd stammer
Hammering the night colourless.

A confusion of night with sound.
A confusion of night with sound.

A confusion of sound with night
Otherwise the realization is completely a gift.

Afraid of adjusting the ribbon
Touch without touching until everyone guesses a winner —

Under the B: Bullfrog Black Blackness.
Earth Stone Naked Jewellery

Tab-keyed night noises. The odd carriage return. Tab tab tab.
The odd carriage   return.

Dark and darker still — words that move downhill to fall
Below sunset that has already kissed so many

Full and hard and fleeting.
Red and orange stains that remember dying

And a locomotive waking up the forest.
Metal-on-metal: a black-letter'd stammer

Hammering the night colourless.
Colouring the night hammerless.

Imagine being so awake in the forgetting.
I swear it's all true.

I swear it's all true, it's all true, all true, all true.
Especially when there's nothing but metal-on-metal-on-metal-on-
metal-on-metal. Could there be more
than twenty-two?

Left to our Own Devices

Postcard Town

Light snow is coming down
Mountains piled up all around
Train whistle blows its lonesome sound
And pulls into this postcard town

On the train — four days in
Tracks behind you show you where you've been
Up ahead in the night —
A story waiting to take flight

It's the constant motion that's held you steady
This is you're stop but you're not quite ready
You formed a family — made some friends
But this is where that story ends
This is where that story ends

Light snow is coming down
Darkness piled up all around
Train whistle blows its train whistle sound
And pulls into this postcard town

You haven't reached your destination
And still you get off at this station
Test the wind see which way it's blowing
And walk into the next unknown …

Another Song

You're the reason I find myself needing another song
Just another song — wondering what went wrong

Darkest season wet snow bleeding
Through another song — and the road we're on

Windshield weather we were blown together
All night long — listening for the song

It was the blind leading the blind but we didn't mind
The blind leading the blind but we didn't mind
No we didn't mind
No we didn't mind

Now our blue kite has blown away
No strings attached on this windy day
We didn't need it anyway
It was just another song

Remember summer heat cool beneath the sheets
The whole night long — Beautiful crazy song
This love and how it felt — hot enough to melt
Into a lake of stars — tiny lights at a beachside bar

Now with the late season dying and all of this trying
It doesn't feel so strong — not like a lover's song
Some things right and some things wrong
Is this a lover's song?

It was the blind leading the blind but we didn't mind
The blind leading the blind but we didn't mind
No we didn't mind
No we didn't mind

Courage to Spare

Give us courage to love — Courage to spare
And please don't forget to give us prayer
Courage within — Courage without
Courage beyond the shadow of a doubt
Beyond the shadow of a doubt

Quiet our minds — Open our hearts
Help us to love — Help us to start

Give us courage and hope — With strength to spare
A tiny glimpse of truth laid bare
Love within — Love without
Love beyond the shadow of a doubt
Beyond the shadow of a doubt

Open our hearts — Quiet our minds
Help us to love in these difficult times

Give us courage to love — Courage to spare
And please don't forget to give us air
Courage within — Courage without
Courage beyond the shadow of a doubt
Beyond the shadow of a doubt
Beyond the shadow of a doubt

On My Way to Your House

On my way to your house — on my way to you
Distant lights from houses as I drove on through

I'm coming home to you

The blackened fields — The Canadian Shield
Farm house shadow — so much that we don't know

I'm coming home to you

On my way to your house — on my way to you
Music fills the spaces — back road 'Kind of Blue'

Black spruce silhouette — the moon climbs without a net
Orion hunts but not quite yet

I'm coming home to you

The truth is polishing the stone
The truth together and alone
Star-wheel in a summer sky
The first star to remember you by
I'm coming home to you

The blackened night — Disappearing tail lights
Dreams and stars and satellites

I'm coming home to you

On my way to your house — on my way to you
Shadows sweep the front porch — pale moon shining through

And all of this is true

The heat of the trip
The curve of your hip
The kiss from your lips

The Dark Road Loves the Lover

I heard you took a lover just because he lives next door
Your bodies that much closer to the corner store
I am further down the road and the road is getting longer
And there's nothing that I'm owed here
But there's nothing that feels stronger
Than the distance that you're putting between yourself and my love
You used to pull me in but now your push has come to shove

The dark road loves the lover — the dark road loves the love
The dark road loves the lover — the lover, the lover

You say you want something dangerous
You stand there deep in shadow
On your knees now in the dark — any way the wind blows
Someone a little tougher maybe someone to force your hand
Someone a little rougher make you take it like a man

The dark road loves the lover — the dark road loves the love
The moon gets chewed up by the clouds
The night goes undercover

I used to slide in right beside you — close as we could fit
With room for love and room for fear — bit by bit by bit
Skin-on-skin breathing you in — right there deep inside you
Naked to see who you might be — you didn't have to hide you

I heard you took a lover just because he lives next door
Your bodies that much closer to the corner store
I am further down the road and the road is getting longer
And there's nothing that I'm owed here
But there's nothing that feels stronger
Than the distance that you're putting
Between yourself and my love
You used to pull me in but now your push has come to shove

The dark road loves the lover — the dark road loves the love
The dark road loves the lover — the lover, the lover

Waiting for the Next Best Thing to Come Around

You're big city in a small town
Hanging around the lost and found
You're a small fish in a big pond
A sold sign sitting on the front lawn
You're going up you're coming down
Waiting for the next best thing to come around

You're a big noise in a small band
Getting used to the lay of the land
A blue note on a sliding scale
A wet blanket at a fire sale
You're going up you're coming down
Waiting for the next best thing to come around

A quiet bit of desperation
A curious kind of contemplation
An unreliable sort of narration
Marks the loudness of your destination

You're a shrill voice in a loudspeaker
You call yourself a truth seeker
You're full screen without the sound
Waiting for the next best thing to come around

The next best thing — The next best thing
A forgotten song the angels sing
The next best thing. The next best thing
Flying blind with a broken wing

You're plaid pants with a checkered past
You start first but you finish last
A small circus looking for a town
Waiting for the next best thing to come around

You're going up you're coming down
Waiting for the next best thing to come around

Lyrics: GW Rasberry
Music: Rob Unger

Metal Train

It's a metal train with wings for wheels
So this is how the darkness feels
It's a metal train with just one car
The pilot knows just who you are

Don't try to make me say what this song might be about
Don't try to make me say cuz the truth just might come out
Don't try to make me say — don't try to make me say
Don't try to make me …

It's a metal train that's gone too far
The last one leaves the door ajar
It's a metal train the wings are black
It's a one-way flight — it won't come back

Don't try to make me sing another happy protest song
Spell out all the words so the crowd can sing along
Don't try and make me sing — don't try and make me sing
Don't try and make me …

Yet the gift comes by default without understanding
To know that a crash is also a landing

A jack-knifed rig a punctured moon
Midnight at the break of noon
Trip through the cloudbank and still climbing
The fuse is lit — the rest is timing

So pick a war — pick any war
And wonder what it started for
We were on that train the day it flew
We saw it burn and we all knew

Don't try to ask us why the planet spins this way
Don't try to ask the crowd the crowd's not talking anyway
Don't try to make us say — don't try to make us say
Don't try to make us …

Lyrics: GW Rasberry
Music: James Campbell, GW Rasberry, Rob Unger

Gasoline, Guitars, Groceries & Guns

Gasoline, guitars, groceries & guns
There's nothing new under the sun
Shop until you drop—it's 4 in one:
Gasoline, guitars, groceries & guns

Upstate New York—not far from the border
Music, commerce, law and order
In the land of red, white and blue
Saw the sign—could it be true?

Gasoline, guitars, groceries & guns
Be sure not to miss out on all the fun
Sons tell your fathers—fathers tell your sons
Gasoline, guitars, groceries & guns

Ammunition and nutrition
An All-American tradition
God help the human condition

Gasoline, guitars, groceries & guns
Gasoline, guitars, groceries & guns
Gasoline, guitars, groceries & guns

With Rob Unger

Emily & Eric (Late Night Amsterdam)

Emily & Eric — together so fine
They mixed some smoke in with their wine
Took some honey with their moon
Through coloured glass and shiny spoon

Met them both in Amsterdam
It was a smaller part of a bigger plan
We moved like air through a ceiling fan
On a rain-soaked night in Amsterdam

The power of sex — the beauty of skin
Their tattoo'd love was built right in
Narrow canals — brick and black water
The music box that Eric bought her

The gig becoming transatlantic
Everything here for the hopeless romantic
The red-light glowing talismanic
Every secret wish granted

Met them both in Amsterdam
It was a bigger part of a smaller plan
Found ourselves in a late-night jam
Going down in Amsterdam

Ça me Fait Penser (It Makes Me Think)

My life n'est pas trés difficile
Just the light here on the windowsill

My life n'est pas trés importante
Toutes les choses that I don't need but want

Toutes les choses that I don't need but want
My life n'est pas trés importante

Ma vie n'est pas trés difficile
Mais quelque fois that's how it feels
Oui, quelque fois that's how it feels
Just the light here on the windowsill

Quest-ce-que c'est?   C'est vrai   Ça me fait penser

Ca me fait penser that right and wrong
Are verses of the same chanson

It makes me think — It makes me think
Each life a song drawn out in ink

Je sais Je sais Je sais pourquoi
Je cherche le needle dans le straw

Je sais je sais je sais pourquoi
Golden vineyards comme c'est la

Perhaps that's why I choose to stay
Ou peut-etre c'est pourquoi I can not say

Ce que je veux dire
Plus loin et trés, trés near
Plus loin et trés, trés dear
Ce que Je veux dire

In a booth at Heaven's Restaurant
My life n'est pas trés importante

Sticks & Stones

Sticks and stones may break my bones but names can never hurt me
I'm here on loan 'till no one's home and breath and bone desert me
And breath and bone desert me

Day is done gone the sun — the earth and stone are sleeping
Day is done there is no one who'll pray my soul for keeping
Who'll pray my soul for keeping?

It's a dark song I saved for you
Sometimes don't know who I'm singing to
Who to forgive and what to forget
How to live with what I haven't lived yet
Sometimes don't know who I'm singing to
It's a dark song I saved for you

Down on my hands and my knees in the dirt
Mud on my shoes a rip in my shirt
Every song I've ever known
Whispered as a graveside poem

Sticks and stones and buried bones you're now forever sleeping
We lowered you down into the ground the earth & stone for keeping
The earth and stone for keeping

I loved you then I love you now — a promise here I'm keeping
I loved the best way I knew how — the earth and stone for sleeping

Left to Our Own Devices

Left to our own devices — I'd be herbs and you'd be spices
You'd be solve and I'd be crises — left all on our own
We'd be more we'd be less — you'd be certain I'd be guess
I'd be guilt — you'd confess — left all on our own

Left all on our own
Noses to the grindstone
Grab the handle — grab the wheel
Go by goodness — go by feel
Everything we've ever known
Left all on our own

You'd be naked I'd undress — I'd be stroke you'd caress
Less and more and more or less — left all on our own
You'd be talking 'bout the time — I'd be waiting for the rhyme
We'd be turning on a dime — left all on our own

You'd be   I'd be   We'd be
As long as you'd come see me
A bit of false a bit of true
You know I'd do it all for you
Left here on our own

Spring eternal Fall behind — Winter weighing on your mind
Every season has its time — left here on our own
Never thrilled but never boring — Summer now has lost its mooring
All the after and before-ing — left here on our own

Left all on our own
Noses to the grindstone
Grab the handle — grab the wheel
Go by goodness — go by feel
Everything we've ever known
Left all on our own

Song for Norah Jones

Every time I pick up the phone
I hear a song by Norah Jones
Beautiful voice beautiful face
Atmospheric silk and lace

Grounded earthy denim too
Easy listening slightly blue
And oh that voice that Norah voice
As if listening were a choice
Lifting songs from the earthly plain
And lightly touching down again

Yet jealousy gets me nowhere
Trying to avoid her dark-eyed stare
The Norah Machine is everywhere
Money-dusted promotional fare

It seems Nora Jones has caught up with the Rolling Stones
Or Willie Nelson's aging bones
The Beatle's lovely distant niece
Everybody wants a piece — of Norah Jones

That first album everyone buys
Even the posters are life-size
Don't stare too deeply into those eyes

Easy to love not to like
The cover girl behind the mic
But then again I shouldn't whine
About all the time I stood in line

My studio debts, bills and loans
All paid off by Norah Jones …

Patron Saint

Everybody wants a Patron Saint
An old coat of arms — a new coat of paint
Everybody wants some money in the bank
Some food on the table — some gas in the tank

Everybody wants — Everybody needs
Everybody loves — Everybody bleeds

Everybody wants a kick at the cat
Everybody wants to know where it's at
Everybody wants to make a new start
Everybody wants to sing from the heart

Everybody wants — Everybody needs
Everybody wants to do a good deed

Do something good maybe turn it around
From the biggest of cities to the smallest of towns
They do it for love — they do it for fear
Such a short time we get to be here

Everybody wants to feel some love
Everybody wants to be part of
Part of the loving — part of the loved
Part of the loving — part of the loved

Everybody wants a Patron Saint
A new coat of arms — an old coat of paint
Everybody wants to make a new start
Everybody wants to sing from the heart
So let's start …

Wintergreen Studios Press is an independent literary press. It is affiliated with the not-for-profit educational retreat centre, Wintergreen Studios, and supports the work of Wintergreen Studios by publishing works related to education, the arts, and the environment.

www.wintergreenstudios.com

www.ingramcontent.com/pod-product-compliance
Lightning Source LLC
Chambersburg PA
CBHW071238090426
42736CB00014B/3135